# Free Verse Editions

Edited by Jon Thompson

# THE BODIES

Christopher Sindt

Parlor Press
Anderson, South Carolina
www.parlorpress.com

Parlor Press LLC, Anderson, South Carolina, 29621

Library of Congress Cataloging-in-Publication Data

Sindt, Christopher.
 The bodies / Christopher Sindt.
  p. cm. -- (Free verse editions)
 ISBN 978-1-60235-285-8 (pbk. : alk. paper) -- ISBN 978-1-
60235-286-5 (ebook)
 I. Title.
 PS3619.I54785B63 2012
 811'.6--dc23
                                        2012000366

Cover design by David Blakesley.
Cover: Commuters Castro Valley © 2010 by Jessica Dunne.
 Painting photographed by Ira Schrank. Used by permission.

Printed on acid-free paper.

Parlor Press, LLC is an independent publisher of scholarly and
trade titles in print and multimedia formats. This book is available
in paperback and ebook formats from Parlor Press on the World
Wide Web at http://www.parlorpress.com or through online and
brick-and-mortar bookstores. For submission information or to
find out about Parlor Press publications, write to Parlor Press,
3015 Brackenberry Drive, Anderson, South Carolina, 29621, or
e-mail editor@parlorpress.com.

# Contents

# THE BODIES

All things that are found on the earth go by the names of elements of natural [bodies].

—*Carl Linnaeus*

Each art must use its tools; each soul its body.

—*Aristotle*

# Beginning with a Line from *Exodus*

*And daubed it with slime*
*and pitch, and put the child therein.*
A particular pitch, a daring
daub, he floated
among the cradles,
he floated to.  Remember
the bodies

and a bauble, selved
with slime and pitch.
The child floated to.
Sinecured
to false heavenly, a birth
mark.  To be a
possibility therein, pirated

pitch, a version.
Locusts come later; now,
he looks like someone's
child there among
the rushes. To be
daubed, appear as
what he's done.

## Coast Live Oak

The oak has a language in it.
A buzz, a veiling buzz

      insists on the *I wish*.

If you wish, the oak is buzzing, not
from swarming, simply alarming,

      the dogs *inflecting*

inside their boxes and chains.
Listen, listen through.

      I have lost the *I have*.

I carry a card to unlock forbiddens,
a silent card that *screams*.

In the true heart of Sunday
the grass reforms its composite

      self, screaming *menace*,

claimed in substrate,
the step-

child of the Chronicler.

It won't speak grammatically.
It will impose green throughout

      and lie down for the *mower* again.

(She is remembered

only in daydreams, *never*

in speech, never around the students,
never at the ballpark while the players

trot the bases before the game.)

These flat recollections of events
rarely feel like living.

And these children
bombing and standing beneath bombs.

This secretary,

these defenses
and this televised citizenry.

This oak and its technicolor translation.

# Hayward Marshlands

Star was darting, prying specs of light along levees. Hear me here tomorrow and the next day, get the body in place. And everything that follows: calf, nape, and small. Let the bodies be assembled along levees, let them make salt.

Past the recycling plant, past the blasted shoreline. In the broken made world, words fall between us.

Airplanes on their southern approach to Oakland, concrete wind, a grey sheet. Shy and pneumatic, the distance between shore and shore. The glance can't fix underwater, even in the shallows. When I knew you best, you were crying straight, but usually you were darting and masking. Hear me tomorrow in the red marsh grass. We will agree, and the water will be different, slightly on the surface and slightly underneath, driftwood.

# Beginning with a Line by Rilke

*Just once; no more*

The ash
And its competent leaves
Just once

Above the wetland
Once the ridge
Laden, no more

Fog as flower
No more
The baying Holsteins

How the sun
Closes, happy
The ash, happy

The holsteins no more
Heron are you happy
Heron are you just

# Ground Problem

The previous     (planning as)     ("natives")

and deer-resistant          (smile
violet)                    withering and drawn
losing investment

when mistakes are                    capital
one plant              punishes (paper crèche)
                  birthday problem          press, kiss

                    circles for trees, (trunks)
          cross-hatches making
          steps in space     "you have to imagine three dimensions"

(before you go can I          ask, fear of the unasked) "A bottle of"
(spring) plans
nervous laughter because mistakes

          (tensiled and tearing)          for fear
"growing" more and more

the way you                    want it if you know
in the side view          looking down the drive
path of rock                    (fact: slant, drainage

          issue: clay)          beds of cedar
"may decay quicker but you          don't care"

          spring greens     (major growth spurt)
when the plan calls for messy she sounds
                              worried,

          a drawing-in,   (yardstick)
          a tracing, a temporary version

the sun will tell us                divorced light
a beige and then        a bright            (plant

        palette)
we can't tell here                      "what it will
look like in"            what disasters  (earthquake)

and what        near-disasters between two people
stop talking in metaphors and choose a color
laughter is after and hers.

## Sunset Beach

The ocean is not a dark mirror.


And the beach spreads its minutes largely: driftwood, folding chairs,
apple grass, pelicans


tracing and breaking the breaking surface.


The sun hits the water directly and the world seems briefly
measurable.


Not a dark mirror:      a place for diving     foundation for
becoming.


Before, when the other was listening, speaking was easier.


Unnerving clarity with the sun directly overhead.


How to represent another thing or its feelings.


Or a certain dog or cat that must be named Alice or Scout,
particulars that announce themselves and reach out, or don't,


maddening to others, the way the path of the sanderling must
overlap the path of the sandpiper, for some truly small amount of
time, but historical

still.  Not a dark mirror, knowledge full of seams and breaches: the sandpiper and the sanderling must be

invented again, sometimes together sometimes apart.

When did enormity give way to measurement?

(Someone is always eager to explain.)

Once sand poured in here as the surf washed the sediment back.

When the other was listening, speaking was.

You want to order yourself away from the ocean's will to misremember.

The Ohlone came here to clam.  The sandy hands of the Ohlone while they clammed.

(Off to the side, a boy with a red kite.)

Someone should walk down through the pines and ask you to coffee or a late lunch.

Someone should appear on the beach with a video camera and five or six sharp pencils.

Foundation for becoming, underwater dictation, screeching gulls,
your great loves and dislikes.


(Now the historians cheer and fly their kites.)


Once this place was a rancho.  Joaquin Castro planted the cypresses
that line the main road.


Within the ocean's voice lies one perfect version of the story


no one can remember.  Or the future is the place to better
remember: the future doesn't needle


like the past: it is lovely until perhaps just before it arrives.


Acting as the self flickers and disappears (goodbye self!), or becomes
temporarily brand new.


When the other was listening, speaking.


After statehood, Leslie Kester bought the land for $10 down,
mortgage to $27, 500, planted eucalyptus, raised cattle and
chickens on the eastern slope of the dunes.


The hiss of the eucalyptus.


Not a dark mirror:      for planting      for perfect vision and
grammatical mistakes.

Crab life, mollusks, and further beneath: sea urchins, mushroom coral, lantern-fish.

(Refrain: a place for diving, foundation for becoming.)

"The two-mile dip into the oceanic abyss ends at a seafloor that is featureless but for granite outcroppings, shale reefs, or the remains of shipwrecks."

The shallow structure is written in waves.

Harry Hooper, an outfielder for the Red Sox, bought part of Leslie Kester's farm in 1925 and called it Sunset Beach.

You're worried you may not understand, and your questions have been overlooked.

In 1929 they began to build houses on the bluff: first the Lyons then the Snyders, the Pages, the Bleshes, the Rosses and the Wilsons.  Frank Ross ran a diner at the bottom of the hill.

Needing things to be sung around the campfire.

A foundation        lacking reflection.   Shipwrecks.

Dusk now, and the curlews run along the beach with their long beaks and Napoleon legs: godwits and gulls, smashed up bits of shell.

(The hiss when I say *eucalyptus*)


Looking down and away from the sunset, a sky without fretfulness,
reflecting wholly what the viewer lacks in his enormous failings.


They planted dune grass and apple grass and sea fig, Monterey pine,
Arizona blue cedar, pyracantha.


(When the other was listening)


The beach was a POW camp during the second world war, and
every year, three or four clam diggers would drown.


The line between water and sky deepens        : symbol for slippage.


And in another place you rode your Schwinn the two miles down
Bell Road to Dewitt Cinema and paid fifty cents for *The Love Bug*,
or *The Goose that Laid the Golden Egg*.


How many other people were there too, ordering themselves
around the joys and sorrows of 1979.


You like to remember it as a large tracking shot.


It reaches up above the cinema and follows the boy on his journey
past the moto-cross track and the elementary school to the pastures
and the county jail, the asylum and the condo complex and the
softball fields

and on and on, widening.

(Not a dark mirror               a foundation of)


The tidy efficiency of the hundreds of wooden stairs that lead up and away from the beach.


Sturdy, well-wrought stairs, made by someone not yesterday, not the day before, but when,


when.

# Beginning with a Line by Wallace Stevens

*It is fatal in the moon*
*and empty there.*
Fatal lake, empty lake
children's voices, Rock Lake.
Blossoms in the moon
blossoms curling.
It is a cup, a cup
across the lake.  Delay, fatal

in the lake and empty.
Fatal in the
mountains. Empty depths
in empty blues and greens.
The moon's royal,
the green plaids of fatal.
Empty pines
standing in the moon.

The mountain
quietly empty above.
Wet dog framed by green
rocks framed by fatal.
Buzz went the flies
quiet quiet goes Rock Lake.
Shrill shrill goes the hawk.
And below are fields of punished yarrow.

# Death Valley

Pupfish
Swimming in their own
Warm pools

Shoshone poisoned
Nothing
Left but salt

91% of the wetlands
Stolen and what's left
Chalky rocks

Alluvial fans
They've built a museum
To deceit

The earth
Pounding
Like unbalanced laundry

Rocky detritus
With aprons on
Avoiding news

That isn't poetry
The flood rolls its debris
Onto the floor

Like gift wrapping
You are
Standing on the story

# Fishing after Breakfast

If you stand next to the lake
you will soon be losing

your voice. Rosy-finches lift
their heads and say nothing.

Say nothing, seize the water as
their own. Your urge to speak

forgets its message. Something about
being *in contact with me.*

Are you in contact with me?
You want access to the mysteries,

the revelation of speech come to tease
the hunger of arms and legs? You're

next to the Lake of Our Dreams
not in the Lake of Our Dreams, again,

and in the morning the hissing
chemical warmth of the camp stoves.

Beside the ponderosas you're bristling
with nothingness, the needles beneath

your feet like an undertow, the land
of sides and the black hole of ins.

Down trees all around like backdrop, granite
framing the lake like a choke-collar.

Why is the promise of clarity
the wrong promise? Clarity is
a garment. The urge is elsewhere.

# So and So as a Force of Nature

Bounded by willow, as is
the way in field guides: the river
channeling, ebbing, as a story

returns, roaring more, then
less, cascading and flattening: or,
between: the place

of a story: a man fishes, swims, falls
into, speaks from: or
a kind of mirror, found in pools

beside eddies, the other side of
the canyon rising, to view
the black phoebe as it skims

the surface, the hawk's distorted
arc: you are so clearly
in or out of the river, entirely

missing something that is
underneath, or even, in:
in other rivers, there might be

a god or headwater to speak
of, or a raft, or danger or
solitude: it may lead

somewhere: you may know it
in your words: *cataract, back-*
*flow, anabranch*; or float

through rapids or toward
a dam: the dusty smell of
blackberry, grey pines

softening the hillside, standing
beside for an instant, this one:
coming to an end, attainably:

my river doesn't roar,
it opens to its own
gravity, its exit, listens for
the slight gasp
in time, and fills—

# Shake the World

Leaves channeled me
To the suffering of the lake

Algal swimming with hotel
A mother resting there

I was under for a time
A mother gone for a time

Lakes can be drowned
Here, say goodbye now

By accident we fell into
The scarlet beside her

People, beware of the dams
Small pools move inside larger ones

# Formation

Having accumulated suffering for no purpose
Because of my honoring and serving this body,
What use is attachment and anger
For this thing that is similar to a piece of wood?

—Shantideva, *A Guide to the Bodhisattva's Way of Life*, translated by Stephen Batchelor

# Continental

I was looking for maps        but rocks crumbled
in Drake's Bay      on defensive sand,
a temporary bluff     the waterway
winnowed while    we mealed our grasses
for milk and yogurt   and eased these
crabs down our throats    like curlews
know to do    we moved  like ospreys
circling above     yellow sand verbena
on the disturbed berm    making bright
love to the continental    shelf
to weather     of the Farallones
harsh cry    calm flower

## Salt

Here in the marsh        you "came upon me"
with your attachments        heron, chert
the woman with the first        idea
I'm building a wall        with your granite poses

the sun settles        like a wedding guest
in pastels        we love what chatters
in the wetlands        dear wren
dear sparrow        echoing under-
story with        repetitive notes
your face splinters        under certain pressures

# Without

The octopus          and its tendrils
my field, my fallow          shades
of coiled plastic          foggy gauzings
the viewing          trapped in clarity
shavings          of madrone
along the path          it takes time
to notice          and time to honor


see the blazing          citadel
the arm lacerated          by the blade
the tendriled          knowledge of
the altered          any number of
petals,          dense mass
any family of

# Greenpicker Trail Interlude

Ridge no less
Small meadow at firtop
Planned seedlings
Osprey calls to another
All it has is wind
when alights

One life
Will make three
Each unidentified
Call another cry

Ridge no less
A real ocean, there
You call it an ocean
Of feelings
Waiting to love it

# Power

Returned to the bay          of cattle, limping
electric smile          from a shaken
prominence         roads on all sides
up to water       mountain vision
"opposite and alternate"      sepals and petals
the same color        the spirit world
questions our time    here in the undergrowth
our purpose        our delivery
too deliberate,   self-      imposed as always
flowers dying        in their vases
and littering        the floor

last night I dreamed     of your sweeping

## Made of Cedar

These calls at six a.m.        crowings
in my cage      the blackest
leaf, love of      flocking phone lines
love of sugar    doesn't make you
my hummingbird      "Uranium
enrichment    is the ultimate
symbol of      modernity"
cormorants claim      the fog over Inverness
my anger is      yours
the sun is your      color my princess

# Unmistakably

Baby girl or boy      a sheen
Archeological      through the window
I see the rancher      mowing summer grasses
yes I know sometimes      you think
nothing is happening      despite the evidence

of attachment      our eyes marked
with looking askance      the goldfinch hopping
about the Oregon ash      lasting about
as long as my "bouts"      with fear
the mower moves      *so* slowly
down the row      at these speeds
anyway, the pictures      roll and roll
slideshow

# South of Limantour Interlude

A single godwit looping the beach
Passes clouds on the edge of
relationship to wind, kings

He/she keeps distance
Silt passing, call it sand
No/yes, no/yes, landing

A short time, cloudy god
Deposits of driftwood
Piled like crosses, kings

A traveler with a light touch
Not a diver, not a hunter

# Blue Is What Burns

Re the situation          referred to in your letter
shall we call it          "The Greatest Worries of A"
or "What at Night Can Be          Imagined"?
the flowers are replanted          when they wither
in their beds of straw          Some are waiting
for country buses          under the Milky Way
re my life so far          "Shipwrecks I have Seen or Caused"
with words          grafted and replanted, pretty
words,  fists clenched          this report
I would like to call          "The 3 Known Monocultures of C"


the finch so light on the branch     it seems to lift


the bird is blinded          by what it sees

# Marriage

Becoming birdlike, misted        by advection, dew
point discarded     as reason might be
maturity opens rotting     I think of the tent
in Olema, its musty zipper     "A temporary suture
over the San Andreas fault"     the aluminum
RV's pumping     electricity and water
beneath Douglass firs

the star flower
might speak of human     frailty or question
the two bodies     serving each other
can classification be     denied by its objects
can they name     themselves
the air was colored     black
our skin was     cracking, rifting
reveries over breaching     granite

# Drake's Bay Interlude

Let formations
Take shape
As brown pelicans

If not verbena
Small yellow
And sweet pink

He sees crumbly
He thinks nesting
Conserving

Crabs remain
Perennial
Eggs on tossed seaweed

Harbor seals, feathered feet
Earless Buddhas need their rest

# The Plough

A field, greened             with artifacts
furious energy          metered into blossom
her love          for blueberries, a coursing strength
calls of the sparrow             different in each valley
A flooding          toward solstice
The egret drinks          from the canal
beside the Oregon ash             Her madness can be
a girlish green          I have never
heard her say the word          "plenitude"
despite its obvious charms

# Something Illustrated

Because we're apart        I created a soaring bird
poor wing        must be broken eventually
ceaseless wind the bay        we're breathing
dust through leaves        drawn close
by trailside fatigue        birdsfoot trefoil speaking
in humiliations        and bleeding orange
the daylight        splinting through
the strains        in your blind, a temporary valley
as for the Bishop pine        my burning
hands put to work        pyrophite
the fogged-in        backbone of the ridge
knows neither human        nor bird

## Beautiful Edifice

Singers found            and singers in hand
these Bishops are            welcome stations
you're prizing            ginger, a ballad of epic desire
Rancho Punta            de Los Reyes, California

you think            we've saved enough
soft pastels            but the chalk and the flowers
hardly know            this piece of wood
you don't miss            where you've never been
or do you            tracing
roads and rivers            with your rough calluses
piles in sediment            how many haircuts make you
prettiest, regarded            from right lavender

# Beginning with a Line by Julia Kristeva

*Add to these processes the relations*
*Of the fragmented body:*
Add the relations and
fragment: the processes of
the field: poppies, delphinium, vetch:
they must be catching, little
mirrors: on Easter Sunday
in the fragmented

sun, it's time for
cool messages under blue oaks:
globe lilies stand around
with their burdens: irises reveal
their embarrassing frailty:
we must add to these processes
the relations between the partial
sight-lines forward and back:


flowers hate us but we can't stop
listening for their deaths
and resurrections: keep the fragments
when there is no listing, no lasting:
their bodies stand there looking
insolent and too busy: once,
there were no signs in the field:
now the field is ruptured.

# Mercy General

Butterflies spill from the electrocardiograph
       spiders crawl from the surgical tape
under the Virgin Mary I prayed to
       around the heart, we found the grandest sapphire
and we think his name may be next
       in the closet-like hospital church
my brother quite hollow beside
       with great blue herons, a lighter gray
the candles, the cheeks, thimbles
       stitched in, the emergency
of wine, thimbles of bread, bloody body
       register, the names of other attacks
bloody mess on the bathroom floor,
       still living but much collapse, the doctor
my mother says not for me to know directions,
       confirms, the avenues of blood
which elevator, which wing, which way
       closed off, partial, wrong,
to the crinkly sanitary paper and medicine bottles,
       and by my side, crying in the car,
the chemists with their typewriters
       she fingers the white plastic bag
nurses tidying the rooms, disinfecting,
       full of his belongings: pajama bottoms,
keys to cabinets, rolls of gauze,
       pamphlets for the wives of the diseased,
the pain is still, he says to her,
       the grade school diagram of the heart,
while she removes his plastic dinner plate
       the arteries in question laid out like a delta,
the family coming together in the face of
       his finger pointing to the natural flow,
emergency, they know their way by now
       and then to the blockages, the stents,

to the waiting room, coming together
       the diversion tunnels that let the blood flow
in the long pauses, sharing mints,
       cut beneath the river, artificial,
watching the waiting room zenith, reading
       dry land where water should flow, black
the Sunday paper, cell phones going off, and the others
       and the wet sheen of the cat scan,
in the commissary, uncomfortable with sandwiches
       my finger would stick if I touched it
we are made to prefer the tending to the pain

# Scan

Turning to what she attends, as if voice were mist, soundtrack of
    her sweetness.
Receding, her tongue and yours form right foundation, travel with
    different lighting.
Attentions to circumference: silent spaces, pressures, and points of.
Without words: stories limning her temples.
Outside the screen, speech acts injure ideas of flowers and bicycles.
*The tiny muscles around the eyes*, softening through closed lids,
    childhood kaleidoscopes.
Brightness in the jaw, dismantling her feeling of source;
    evaporation, too, a discipline.

Stitches of breath, dank summer laundry in the nose and mouth.
Welcome her headlong swallowing.
Condensed in knowledge of pain, muscled feelings with sides on all
    sides.
Each finger like a petal that throbs and reddens, a system for
    sobbing gushes.
Space beyond the hands, what we might call "the world" or
    "heaven."
Toxins released from their cells, lovers of privacy.
The *heart which began beating* turns toward that beginning.

A household god, left for central worshipping.
Your weaver creates nostalgia for electric pain, training tables.
Pelvis like a blossom that sinks deeply into blue Hades.
Her precise walking, as in children's intentions.
Her eddies of extension, unions beneath cloth.
Many bones come to mind, the feet in their sandals, Jesus.
Word for body bleaching here against gravity.

# The Limits

Whereupon the master said, "If you break off
      a little branch from any one of these plants,
      the thoughts you have will also be broken off."
So I stretched out my hand a little way,
      and broke, from a great thornbush, a small twig;
      its branch called out, "Why have you broken me?"

                    *—Dante*


   The branch bleeds
   so that a soul can speak

                    *—Michael Palmer*

# Invisible Habit

You think I'm not pleased
with the branch
that bleeds?

You think I don't care
about the outside
world, how it must

borrow from
its changings for me?
I like the hemlock,

poison's namesake—
not some syrupy maple—

spiraled needles
that twist out in prongs
like jousting spears.

Too  much violence?
I hate the body when it watches
t.v.  The blood

drawn for me
and invisible habit:
sometimes even the tree

forgets its own
vegetable growth;
then it bleeds and remembers.

# The Dark Inside

You come to me with three lives
and seven secrets.  Petals
wait to fall from the magnolia—

pink splendor, winter
in the provinces, glory
bruised with blight.

Hip and socket, model
of anatomy.  You smell
like peppermint

and salt, something
sprinkled, dashed.
Swing a plaster limb

at me, wrap your arms
around my legs
that are not here.

Make an incision,
maze of organs, hard
and smart as dictionaries.

You're glad I'm honest.
I think I'm better.

I glean sincerity from the dark
inside you.  I lie
until it hurts so much it's real.

# (Hidden Bodies: Note to the Soul of the Maple

I found you in late summer
in a small grove
wrapped in hiddenness,

stoic in exterior,
a slight burning
within, an in-dwelling

consumed with volatile
beginning.  I loved
how you allowed

the young birch
to sprout from
your rotting

center, allowed it
to find its body
in yours.  Once, I thought

I could love a tree—
this was the inquisitive,
experimental me—

pick one
and make the switch,
transmigrate to pine,

laurel—be wooden,
possessed, be Daphne.)

# The Borders

You sat on the border
of sun and shade, you fell
into the den of another.

The soul's lot:
to hover around suffering
and simply not feel

its substance.
Things happen far away
to people you don't know

and they touch me
in waves, like knife-tips.

If I could say only one thing:
you cannot live without
the grief of others.

(A cricket inches
along the staircase
and decides not to fall.)

You wonder
about the beginning, how
I recall the birth

of my own being—
It was good, and
there was suffering there.

# Science Fiction

All that scares me
is the Milky Way—
it pours past human

sight, locates the limit
of horizon.  I am only
my definitions: everlasting,

burning long and quiet.
When spaceships pass
the stars' souls

look down and laugh,
remembering mosquitoes and jet skis
from their time on earth.

On a clear night
you can walk out to the dock
and see the trapeze of starlight

on the water's surface,
the bowl of the sky collapsed,
the way the soul is collapsed by the body.

You want darkness?—
You want the cosmos?—

Not under, outer world,
lost in a forest, like Dante,
dark and holey, tricky, like chess.

# (Monument: Note to the Soul of the Body's Lover

I know you like to watch.
I've felt you
there at the den of

frenzy.  Yes, the body has
a rough, exterior
beauty; it pleases

me too, the outward
curve like a monument
to earthliness, but

his embarrassing desire
to contain another,—

you must teach the body
to see the invisible
you, look off

toward the lake,
not into the water beyond
the water, not into the body

beyond the body.
You think I'm obsessed
with boundless limitation?

No one knows desire
like the soul
trapped in matter.)

# The Temporary World

I've thought too long
on bone and tissue,
mitochondria, DNA,

tried to unveil
your mystery,
your bright seeing

of things: how you loved
the roots of the down tree
(how they reached out

in all the wrong directions),
your voice
when you say *texture,*

*equivalent, tamarack,*
the falling into
the well of another,

what springs
from the temporary

world, the way desire
takes human shape,
sorrow is caged, grief boxed,

and the rest reaches out, boundless
over the surface of the lake,
flattening sinew, forgotten cell.

# Looking Up

(Those stupid stories
of prisoners wanting back in…)

We walked in thicket
by a small waterfall
under a darkening sky.

We seemed to know each other
there: you looked up
to the grove of young hemlocks

and I dwelt in the lake,
aimless sailboat,
lost oar.  Shadows everywhere,

but we tried not to notice
the souls drifting about.
You were polite, divining

the new growth
beside a down maple,
little red hearts

sprouting off—
The body of the tree
meant nothing)

Once, there was despair.
Then, we were turned inside out
and worn by our own garments.

# Little Dusks

But how to look outside
for help: the terror
in the diamond-head,

the possibility
in the water lily.
Some bodies are just bodies,

you must leave them
to love their thick shadows.
And I loved that other

when it came through the door,
loved its way of letting
the soul drift about inside…

After dinner we flick the switch
and little dusks look up
from the edges like cave light.

Perhaps what we need looks up
as we deliver a glass of wine
to the table, looks up,

as the soul knows to do
before blooming,

as the flickering
body calls out
from the edge of the lake.

# Garden

Morning fog, my leavened
birds, what's credential

for you and certainty
for her?  I am smaller

than I feel.  Laws of lips, laws
of hair, laws of where, and

where are the immutable
laws of legs and arms?

Let the story smolder
till the earth is spherical.

To speak of love
that hardened and left,

a plea,
oppressed, a sea of

authoritarian lack.  What
will stack dominion

on adam and eve?
The sea is a garden and

the earth made of feelings.

# Hymn to the God of Dailiness

You dropped through the fiery reaches through the oceans
and the million practical skies.  It is not shadowed

not completely until extinguished until it has lost
all recognition of its previous, its self-

in-the-beginning self.  Outside, the live oak hangs
over the rosemary.  Barbed, obedient limbs.

How rich the world is.  The sad little blue
blossoms seem to speak a kind of song

in your honor.  I think they may be chanting
over and over the word *dazzling*—

meaning, you are full of splendor, full of deceit.

# Beginning with a Line by H.D.

*Smouldering—or rather*
*now bourgeoning.*
Bourgeoning or
rather.  Out of
the pyre in spring.
Smouldering but
after what. It burned
in winter, in a storm,

in a dense thicket
of pines and cypresses,
burgeoning. The trees leave
a grown remnant.  Or rather
rather now now now—
She was smouldering
when she came
to know me when

she came
to burgeoning, or rather
when we came to
I'd rather now, I would
rather now, I would
rather smoulder
now, I would rather
I would rather now smoulder.

# Beginning with a Sentence by Jack Spicer

*And the bodies entangled and yet*
*not entangled in sleeping.*
And the cars entangled
and yet not unforgettably, what,
mangled, the boy
pulled out and bloody,
metal not meant
to touch that.  And in the night

the bodies touch less
than they do in dreams.
Nothing is ever not entangled,
never a lessening.
A dumb fantasy that
anything ever becomes less.
Nothing ever not either
entangled or not everything

but what it is. When I touch her
in the night sometimes
the weight is crushing, sometimes
she burns in sleeping, so active, in resting,
not in carving, not casting, not running,
no, not drilling, but yet in sleeping
and yet entangled
and yet not the bodies.

# Manzanar

Museum a prison
There will be gates
Cemeteries

Beside no relation
Stations and orchards
Temples, perimeters

To dream design
Clouds circling and darkening

Your grandfather's
Plane crashes
In Japanese theater

Your father's nearly deaf
Voices we don't know
A yearning chorus

Never known
At times widowed
Or orphaned

Not held at gunpoint
Have ever
Pledged allegiance

# The Circle

Ever since man has learned to give each part of the body a name, the body has given him less trouble.

—*Milan Kundera*

## To Partake of the Body

*The head is most divine and dominates all the parts within us.* The parts most divine within us display themselves like rotting teeth. I knew the color of her shirt had changed through many washings. All the revolutions in her head! Midsummer at the coast, direct light on assembled bodies for hours before total domination. But the ordering of parts within us going about its business during a blue decapitation. My torso knew her arms and hands in late June in the first days of my body's thirty-sixth year. Shirts and underwear spinning in the washing machine. Divine inside the head, a possum lay murdered on the median, quiet as stock footage. Why has one body been handed to another for noticing? When we were partaking of each other, she said *both arms please.* The day sounds like galloping.

/Plato, *Timaeus*/

# Form of

*The soul cannot be without a body, while it cannot be a body; it is not a body but something relative to a body.* A body is my relative today, and at the cutting board with a view of the summer garden it cannot be my fingertips and wrists. The train scraping slowly down valley, a body that cannot be, movement without soul, not a body but something moving and now gone. The towhees scratching at the grasses after the sprinklers have ceased, their muscled breasts bursting their bodies. The soul cannot be moved away from. A body cannot be without. It is not a body for me to say but something relative. Relative of bees. Soul without hive.

/Aristotle, *On the Soul*/

# Supply

*Nature has created the auricles as storerooms placed close to the heart.*
The shadowy corners of the storeroom. My creation: the blood issues
from corners we carry. We were created and placed close. Created,
it *issues* from the corners of the room, shadows from the man and
woman among their creations of words and volume. Creation is
singular first. Auricles: once the heart speaks, the blood's journey is
fated, and the waiting stops. Blood is the word. Has: What has issued
from our two bodies and the storerooms we carry in our hearts?
Placed: One travels by bird, the other by sugar. One sits with a heart
made of bone, the other shivers as the blood runs thin. Who? We
trade our shadowy corners. My room, close to the heart. Wherever
go the bodies, nature has.

*/The Epitome of Andreas Vesalius/*

# Song

*She used the otherwise useless and unprofitable expired air as material
for the voice.* It was used for singing. It was used as material for silence,
the sound of a man and woman deciding not to speak. The material
could be manipulated, changed by the parts to be louder and softer,
lessons in speech and diction. He means we sing with our own hot
air, unprofitable. It is true that one woman might find something
useful in this voice that is otherwise useless to another. Invisible,
expired air, dental feelings. The singing of Marlene Dietrich is
forbidden in some households. The phonograph remembers the
moments of expiration. The phonograph has recorded silence that
was useful and profitable. The air enters cold, goes to the heart,
burns, and returns as spirited song. In this way, nature perfected
the body's use and the body's beautiful uselessness. By needing to
breathe the heart and lungs turn a profit with voice. Thus, we go on
breathing and listening to each other. The head might tilt towards
the heavens when it sings. The body grips to the ground as it burns.

/Claudius Galenus, *On the Usefulness of Parts*/

# Lesson in the Scientific Method

*Memory cannot exist without endurance of the things perceived.* The light is bad in the cabin. Sparrows cannot exist outside despite their twittering. It's day, and with endurance things are perceived. Memory grows fond of mountain aster and delphinium. They endure with my pleasure to recall. Whole fields of sunflowers outside the window, blankets of aster, their ways invented now as I write this, their desires so like my own in the decayed endurance. This world exists without our failings to perceive. Once, my beloved, we waited for the flowers to speak their designs, and we existed there, for hours each day, your notebook on your lap, your magnifying glass. So many days divining the field, irises, buttercups, fiddleneck, ants crawling over your feet and sandals. And at night, we made pictures of what we saw, the blurry existence of a flower flattened by the mind with wine and music at the kitchen table, a pencil, smeared charcoal, coyotes unseen in the canyon below.

/William Harvey, "On the Manner and Order of
Acquiring Knowledge"/

# The Circle

*It is a matter of necessity that the blood perform a circuit, that it return to whence it set out.* No matter what you say, I will return from whence I set out. Though I want to continue the journey as far as the sea, I will return as a matter of necessity. I set out along the path with buttons strewn along the trail. *Tick tick* performed the buttons. It is a matter of saying "come back" or a matter of saying "I can't not do without." This becomes an explanation. It becomes a circuit, especially when I'm alone with the circuitry. Have we forgotten the blood? Have we forgotten the performance? I wouldn't leave the blood out of this because it travels and doesn't leave. Window frames. Loops. It seems to be a matter of returning, a step and then a twirl and then the glance toward the window and then the oddly patterned screwing of the eyes and then the circuit is complete. The damn luggage doesn't have wheels. The luggage set out along its own journey and I will wait for its recovery.

/William Harvey, *On the Motion of the Heart and Blood in Animals*/

# Experiments in Respiration

*I placed a sparrow under a glass receiver, filled it with common air.*
Read about a man watching a sparrow. He wanted to scrape sticks
together and invent respiration. He was under our glass, a receiver.
*It was a little stupefied.* It was caught, the little sparrow. Outside,
others twittered in the eaves and made love in the common air.
*It began to be agitated.* It began to discover the lack of oxygen. *Its
respiration became laborious and rapid.* Its rapidity was its downfall.
Respiration is labor under glass in a laboratory. So this is the new
world without oxygen. In the renaissance we learned to separate
elements and kill sparrows. The love among birds was laborious and
rapid. *The symptoms of distress increased.* We read that symptoms
increased. Distress under the elms! This dress under the elms with
heavy breathing. Our symptoms are common and examined. *At
the end of fifty-five minutes, it died convulsed.* All it takes is a bird,
a candle, and some mercury. All it takes to kill a bird is a bird.
Convulsed, the feeling is. Stale air, our love is mephitic, one sparrow
might say to another.

> /Antoine Lavoisier, "Experiments on the Respiration
> of Animals and on the Changes Affected on the Air
> Passing through Their Lungs"/

## Some Naturalists

*Nor is there any other, no less fictitious, chain of simultaneous and graded forms, which has its existence only in the imagination of some naturalists, more poets than observers of nature.* Nor is there any poetry. No less fictitious, this existence only in the imagination. The dog sits on the deck looking out on the graded forms: ponderosa, dragonfly, squirrel. There is no simultaneous when we say *simultaneous*, today. Never some naturalists, never poets. Only graded forms along the conveyer with all eyes watching and recording the differences. I'm sorry that poets only ever get it slant. We must travel the land of duplicate forms, hip bone of rabbit chasing after the hip bone of fox. To record my movements tonight along the graded staircase, you must imagine my existence and its fictitious carpeting. That would be ample preparation for union under the forms. There would be poetry in observations of one another. When I lose you, I sit under the tree and imagine that I have found you. You are easier there, under the tree, in fictitious nature. Some naturalists would agree.

/Cuvier, "General Conclusion on the Organization
of Fishes"/

# What Use

*What would be the utility of the sense of feeling, were we not able to turn our hands towards palpable objects?* You may sense today the feeling of the stellar's jay trilling its machine-gun call into a kind of massage along your spine. And the dog ignores the plaintive, high-pitched burst of the chipmunk but looks beyond it toward the palpable highway. Dogs don't have hands, you say. The sense of feeling is toward the world, and we call the world the forest. The forest is palpable to her as setting for movements and smells. The forest must be turned towards. My hands feel useless among the palpable objects, though I feel sometimes as if a string is pulling me further and further into the world we call the forest or the songs of birds. The piercing machine-gun of the jay. It hasn't begun, and it will not end. Were we not able to predict the future, the sun's continual rise into the late-morning, what would be the utility of the objects en route. The palpable objects speak. We hear them with our special faces.

/Cuvier, *Lectures on Comparative Anatomy*/

## Mighty Activities

*There continually reigns throughout the whole of nature a mighty activity, a succession of movements and transformations of all kinds.* A roaring, drunken reign with so much twittering here and there below the cabin, mighty throughout and whole. The mighty reigns and the human maze by the creek's neck allows for all kinds inside and lost. Only the sun and the cloudbank might have a word to say about transformations—they want so badly to just simply STOP. So many eyes in the field, throughout the whole mighty production. The scientists are observed by the mighty kinds! and the notebooks are dropped from cars and lenses crack on the binoculars and we plant a flag for the whole of nature and the mighty activity sits on its throne of water, its throne of leaves. Madness is another word for it. Laughter is yet another. Welcome, all kinds.

/Jean Baptiste Lamark, *Zoological Philosophy*/

# Beginning with a Line by Ezra Pound

*The edge, uncertain, but*
*a means of blending.* Uncertain
proposals, committed
to a means: the edge
not a line but a sea, an area
for blending uncertainty.
The edge, for mingling
within the means

of mind and throat, where
things grow together, know
each other, where
there is enough uncertain
blending, intertidal,
aroused, a means
of hedging, hinging on—
The sea urchin knows

the star fish: when
she knew me, there was
blending. We were
uncertain, the edge
insistent from both
sides, regardless of
what happened
in the budgeting process.

# Beginning with a Sentence by C.P. Dadant, *First Lessons in Beekeeping*

*The beginner will have*
*to use his own judgment.*
The beginner will have
his own will in the scrambled
twilight, and the judgment
its own beginner when blackbirds gust
out of clock-towers beside playing
fields in deep September. Cut grass, roiling

grass beneath judgment, off-season
for beginnings. Whether to split
the hive now, or now, how to read
the swarm. But the beginner has stopped
singing, has exercised judgment. Dully,
the day will have its own water and air,
and remembering is

remembering the blackbirds landing
beside the field above biology lab,
standing for what? Dusky, shivering,
and brittle. You shiver now watching
bombs land on a city on a television
in the hallway of the college's liberal arts
building. The beginner does not have
judgment. The beginner will starve the queen.

# Beginning with a Line by Jackson Mac Low

*Oppressed by gentle*
*disturbances visited hastily.*
Having much to do because
of cause and effect.  An explanation
of state.  Strong words.  Oppressed
by.  Intrigued by.  "Need a slight
movement up the register
for that one there."  Or what about

"needled," so quotidian, the voice,
I am.   Needled by sinuous
exhalations emerged hastily.
Oppressed by gentle visits,
floods and gates, gentle day,
disturbances over there, where
the guests arrive, visited
hastily.  Oppressed by, gentle

brick, to be disturbed
by a visit, a call, to be
so quiet  a visit disturbs, gentle,
gentle, gentle, to be named so
that you must neglect
oppression, visit a disturbance,
break  hastily, make haste,
make wine, make honey.

# Dispersing Surface

Suggestions from the inside alter our perceptions of an "objective" outside.

—*Stephen Jay Gould*

And what you see outside you, you see within.
It is visible and it is your garment.

—"The Thunder: Perfect Mind" in the *Nag Hammadi Library*

Beneath the bridge:          duckweed


frightening
                    the muddy shoreline:

the creek is soupy,
pooling, teasing

                    and kneading words

beside the bank:                    rainbow graffiti
          and infrequently

passing cars: if this were

          destiny, we would stick to ourselves,

where *again* is obvious (as the

creek is obvious

          though diverted):
                                        *mixed in a softer*
                                        *surrounding*


remembering *tears* apart:

          the farmhouse rounded by olive trees, black

stains on the pavement, red
          clay along canals—

          sifted, pressed:

*many of these rocks*
*are highly folded*

the dog running with the horse,                    the lost

leash, an outwardness, the giant bowl
of sky above:

*shows many*
*irregular fractures*

hard to think of anything but injury:
jack rabbits and fence lizards watch from the borders:
I throw seeds into runnels and run away:
the wound not deep enough yet; no, the wound not there at
all—)

the way the horse looks
/*askance*/, memory

locks into an
outwardness askance

to the horse's knowing:
the listener seems
to know, has traveled beside

*composed variously*
*of sheared shale*
*or serpentine*

cottonwood and valley oak:
the trees remembered as

compression,
a layering
on top of the dispersing surface:

*summer heat becomes*
*extreme*

(the wound not deep enough yet)
whereas the rememberer cannot /*hear*/ exactly

on a day in August of the year xxxx:
                             the trailing migrations

of the Nashville warbler, the dusky flycatcher,
western tananger                    (dusky soul, compose me

variously, warble me
              into your fractures):

does the project make it true:
does it make breathing easier:

                         *high enough to keep*
                         *cool marine air from*
                         *penetrating to the*
                         *Great Central Valley*

the story looks like seriousness, here beside
the bridge with mud pooling:

dry, /*difficult*/ and full

              of mustard and radish in spring:
shot from the ground up:

        (we traced the stems of radish up to the petals:
        propellers of veined cloth, as if pressed *before* flowering:
        field mustard: she said the petals were like babies' hands:
        she said they smelled like licorice and talcum powder)

easier, where:

it was supposed to get easier with maps and statistics:

it was supposed to be /*studied*/in this way, become

relative:

shouldn't the layers sometimes reveal

                                    themselves
without work:

    (wild oats: facts gone, drooping panicles, downtrodden:
    you're wondering if consciousness persists there:
    or a word that means consciousness-without-value:
    you're afraid of the upright posture, husk of body,
    body without spirit)

and here the creek and its muddy sop

a kind of                                window,
                  a ragged opening,

yet a /*precise*/ answer

to many                          questions: brown water, blue sky:

    (fog where the mountains should be, and you have so little
      substance today:
    lying in bed, waiting for hours for the elm to take shape:
    inside, a cricket crosses the hardwood and stops at a pair of
      Levis:
    the bush scrapes against the drainpipe; this morning's song:
    blackbirds take flight, their bantam bodies sliding through the
      gray:
            glinting wings finding substance in the air;
            splitting the sky and being denied by the sky)

a single swooping wave                of blackbirds, daily
with cigarettes on the front porch:

                *doesn't look much like it did*
                *thousands of years ago*
                *it has endured*


    (in the absence of thought there is what:
    he felt he could lose the constraints of the body:
    he felt the mind could be collapsed and laid flat)


a wave
and then another wave:

bicycles on the path, hands clutching in March wind,

march wind:

                *the wound not there at all—*

the creek, the seeps, the wetlands turn freeway into
edge:

                *a few are visible*
                *from a speeding car,*
                *but the majority*
                *requires very close*
                *examination*
                *to be appreciated*


and the freeway insists that everything's scenery:

glossy,        summarized:

    (rows of Chinese pistache along the borders, flaring:
    and beyond the pistache, what seems to be an empty distance:
    a loneliness spreading out like a long night:
    the housing developments in Dixon: cut lumber, sticky pavement:

the billboard Holstein, who says in her plywood bubble: My
  milk only 68c a quart):

sometimes I look up to the cloud designs in dreams,

                    sometimees down, water running,

water soaking in:

and yet it always /*presses*/ forward
and disappears, with pretty stupid

          versions of the story trailing behind:

  (it was quiet then, except for the crickets and my pocket
    watch:
  the wound not deep enough yet; the wound not there at all—
  I walked into the field, ran my hand through the safflower:
  felt the prick, the dimpling blood, the soft slow pain):

so that I can return to the bridge:

the mind /*wants*/ this but loves that

                    it never gets this:
hiding among weeds in the aquatic zone:

                              *serpentine plants can be*
                              *lumped into two*
                              *categories:*
                              *tolerators and avoiders*

how shall we explain the:
was established in:
for the protection of the:

*the university*
*has never advertised*

some things, yet, are unseen,
                              publicized: the great

blue heron
with its question mark neck:
poison oak                              promises:

still, something doesn't speak:

nothing                              pretty here,
why should the poetry be:

        (a sky, an emergency room:
        a field of alfalfa insistently, demandingly leveled:
        the raw nerve of the whole world:
        we sewed tomatoes, marigolds, zucchini:
        we dropped snail pellets and pruned roses:
                those were sweet nights! the cats walked by with beautiful
                    sticky tongues and climbed in grape-covered awnings:
                a distant truck, the rolling drone of the combine:
                the soft covering of the place removed: bare cracked dirt:
                later, mourning doves and red-winged blackbirds)

a widening, he feels this

glancing over the field and becoming
                              quarantined
by geography:

                              *covers some 810 square*
                              *miles*
                              *passes through four*
                              *counties*
                              *and forms the border*
                              *between*

this is where the subject empties

and empties: memory deepens

the wound, a floodlight on the fields at night:

and who is knowing this: a map: design: the scars

among the characters seem to be calling out now:

she remarked that             I had lost the ability
to find words for my emotions:

the creek was dammed in 1957: the sky was darkening
                                   when we kissed

beside the creek: things I call
blackbirds were pouring into the sky.

# Ending with a Passage from *Exodus*

Who can answer rightly
the call to be named?

One questions his animals,
and another proclaims an island.

This is my trickling voice,
lost in the ellipsis.

Three blank spaces in the text.
Or, I called out to Moses three times

as the turkey vultures haunted
the grazing Holsteins near Tomales Bay.

And said, the names are birdcalls.
And said, make law from birdcalls.

*And said, Moses, Moses.*
*And he said, Here am I.*

# Acknowledgments

The author gratefully acknowledges the editors of the following publications in which some of these poems first appeared, occasionally in different form: *Free Verse: A Journal of Contemporary Poetry and Poetics*: "Death Valley" and "Garden"; *The Land of Give and Take* (Momotombo Press chapbook, 2002): "The Limits" and "Mercy General"; *Nocturnes:* "Hayward Marshlands," "Beginning with a Line by Wallace Stevens," "Some Naturalists," and "Beginning with a Line by Julia Kristeva"; *Notre Dame Review*: "Fishing after Breakfast" and "So and So as a Force of Nature"; *Pool*: "Hymn to the God of Dailiness"; *Putah and Cache:* "Dispersing Surface"; *Swerve*: "Beginning with a Line by Jack Spicer," "Beginning with a Line by Ezra Pound," "Beginning with a Line by H.D.," "Beginning with a Line from *Exodus*," and "Beginning with a Line by C.P. Dadant, *First Lessons in Beekeeping*"; *Xantippe*: "Form of."

Grateful acknowledgment is made to the following for the gift of space and time to write: Dick Biddle and Cheryl Morgan, The Blue Mountain Center, Mesa Refuge, The Putah-Cache Artist in Bioregional Residency program, Susanna Schroll, and Mark Sindt.

Many thanks to my friends and family who helped in countless ways. Thanks especially to Brenda Hillman. To Leigh Morgan. For my father and mother, James and Mary Sindt.

# About the Author

Christopher Sindt is an Associate Professor of English at Saint Mary's College of California, where he teaches in the MFA Program in Creative Writing and serves as the Vice Provost for Graduate and Professional Studies. He lives in Oakland, California with his wife Leigh, his daughter Halina, and his son Luke. He is the author of the chapbook, *The Land of Give and Take* (Momotombo Press, 2002).

Photograph of the author. Used by permission.

# Free Verse Editions

Edited by Jon Thompson

*13 ways of happily* by Emily Carr
*Between the Twilight and the Sky* by Jennie Neighbors
*Blood Orbits* by Ger Killeen
*The Bodies* by Christopher Sindt
*Child in the Road* by Cindy Savett
*Country Album* by James Capozzi
*The Curiosities* by Brittany Perham
*Current* by Lisa Fishman
*Divination Machine* by F. Daniel Rzicznek
*The Flying House* by Dawn-Michelle Baude
*Instances: Selected Poems* by Jeongrye Choi, translated by Brenda
    Hillman, Wayne de Fremery, and Jeongrye Choi
*A Map of Faring* by Peter Riley
*Physis* by Nicolas Pesque, translated by Cole Swensen
*Poems from above the Hill & Selected Work* by Ashur Etwebi, trans-
    lated by Brenda Hillman and Diallah Haidar
*The Prison Poems* by Miguel Hernández, translated by Michael Smith
*Puppet Wardrobe* by Daniel Tiffany
*Quarry* by Carolyn Guinzio
*remanence* by Boyer Rickel
*Signs Following* by Ger Killeen
*These Beautiful Limits* by Thomas Lisk
*An Unchanging Blue: Selected Poems 1962–1975* by Rolf Dieter
    Brinkmann, translated by Mark Terrill
*Under the Quick* by Molly Bendall
*Verge* by Morgan Lucas Schuldt
*The Wash* by Adam Clay
*We'll See* by George Godeau, translated by Kathleen McGookey
*What Stillness Illuminated* by Yermiyahu Ahron Taub
*Winter Journey* [Viaggio d'inverno] by Attilio Bertolucci, translated
    by Nicholas Benson

CPSIA information can be obtained at www.ICGtesting.com
Printed in the USA
BVOW041026151112

305593BV00001B/21/P